Reading Together

Many Hands
Counting Book

Read it together

The *Many Hands Counting Book* invites children to join in the reading with their hands *and* their voices.

The familiar setting of a playgroup helps children to relate to the story and encourages them to talk about what they know.

Six giving hands.

Apple juice!

The pictures in the book help children to see what the words mean.

Eight squeezing hands – they're having a lovely time!

Squeezing hands!

Children can take part in the story and join in with the actions. By clapping, squeezing and waving as you read the story, they will enjoy being really involved.

Use the *counting* theme in the book to turn reading it into a little game where children try to guess the number on the next page.

... and ten waving ...

hands – bye bye!

One patting hand, Two drawing hands, Three ... stroking hands.

How does it go?

I know another counting rhyme.

Children enjoy talking about the story as you read it and afterwards. They can tell it in their own words or make up their own rhymes and stories.

We hope you enjoy reading this book together.

For Mama with love

First published 1998 by Walker Books Ltd
87 Vauxhall Walk, London SE11 5HJ

This edition published 2005

2 4 6 8 10 9 7 5 3

The text was first published by Brent Young Writers.
© 1998 Brita Granström
Introductory and concluding notes © 1998 CLPE/LB Southwark

Printed in China

ISBN 1-4063-0062-4

www.walkerbooks.co.uk

Many Hands Counting Book

Illustrated by Brita Granström

WALKER BOOKS
AND SUBSIDIARIES
LONDON · BOSTON · SYDNEY · AUCKLAND

1 One patting hand

2 Two drawing hands

3 Three stroking hands

4 Four clapping hands

5 Five shaking hands

6 Six giving hands

7 Seven building hands

9 Nine helping hands

10 Ten waving hands

zero 0
one 1
two 2
three 3
four 4
five 5
six 6
seven 7
eight 8
nine 9
ten 10

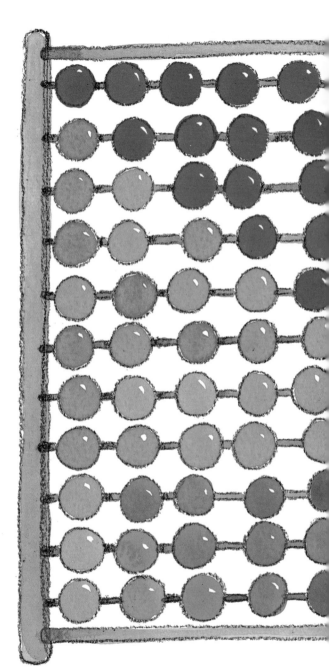

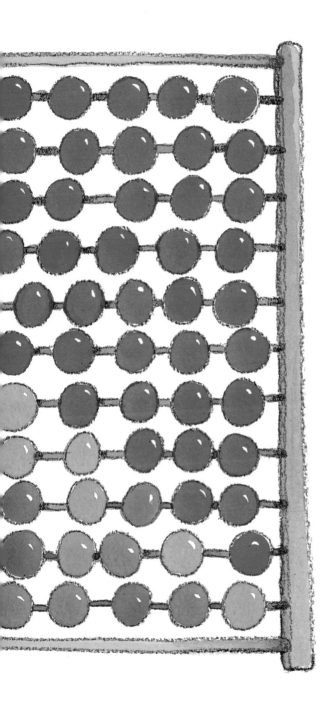

10 ten
9 nine
8 eight
7 seven
6 six
5 five
4 four
3 three
2 two
1 one
0 zero

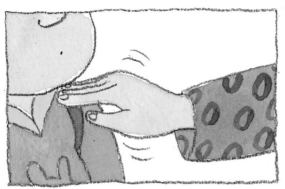

1 patting hand

2 drawing hands

5 shaking hands

6 givi

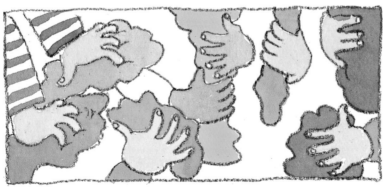

8 squeezing hands

9 helpi

3 stroking hands

4 clapping hands

nds

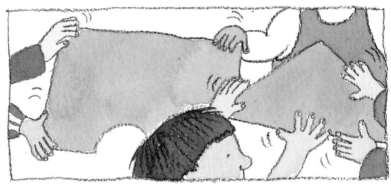

7 building hands

nds

10 waving hands

Read it again

Count the hands

Use the chart on the previous page to count the "helping", "clapping", "building" hands. You could also look through the book together and count the hands in each picture.

Five shaking hands!

One-two-three-four-five hands.

Count to ten

You can use the abacus picture for counting from one to ten and ten to one. It's also good for showing the different ways the number ten is made up.

Make a collection

Children can go on a treasure hunt around the home, collecting toys and other objects to arrange in number order. They could even draw them and make their own counting book.

Two teddy be
What's nex

One ball.

Thre
Three

Act it out

Reading the book again, children can be encouraged to join in with each movement if you lead the way.

Four red and six green make ten.

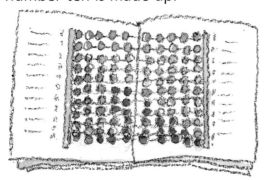

Matching game

You can help your child make different-coloured hand prints, cut them out and stick them on to cards to make a matching game for numbers 1 to 5.

What did you do today?

The book tells the story of a morning spent at playgroup or nursery. You can follow through a typical day for your child and write down and draw all the main events on a chart.

Counting books

There are many counting rhymes and songs to enjoy. Other counting books in the Reading Together series include *Ten in the Bed* and *Over in the Meadow* and there are counting rhymes to be found in *Mother Goose*.